On Your Plate

Milk, Cheese, and Eggs

Honor Head

A+

Smart Apple Media

Smart Apple Media
P.O. Box 3263, Mankato, Minnesota 56002

Printed in the United States

Published by arrangement with the Watts Publishing Group Ltd, London.

Created by Honor Head and Jean Coppendale, Taglines
Design: Sumit Charles; Harleen Mehta, Q2A Media
Picture research: Shreya Sharma, Q2A Media

Picture credits
t=top b=bottom c=center l=left r=right m=middle

Cover Images: Shutterstock and Istockphoto.
Photosky/ Dreamstime: 4, Julián Rovagnati/ Shutterstock: 5, Ene/ Shutterstock: 6, Marie C. Fields/ Shutterstock: 7,
 Spirita/ Istockphoto: 8, Cerlobea/ Dreamstime: 9, Thepalmer, Juanmonino/ Istockphoto: 10, Ivonnewierink/
Shutterstock: 11, Adlifemarketing/ Istockphoto: 12, Markstout/ Dreamstime: 13, Adlifemarketing/ Istockphoto: 14,
Elkeflorida/ Istockphoto: 15, Stevenpepple/ Shutterstock: 16, Vangelis/ Shutterstock: 17, Harrisshiffman/ Shutterstock: 18,
Ayeshawilson/ Shutterstock: 19, Joegough/ Shutterstock: 20, Pålespenolsen/ Shutterstock: 21.

Library of Congress Cataloging-in-Publication Data

Head, Honor.
  Milk, cheese, and eggs / Honor Head.
      p. cm. -- (On your plate)
  Includes index.
  ISBN 978-1-59920-335-5 (hardcover)
 1. Cookery (Dairy products)--Juvenile literature. 2. Dairy products--Juvenile literature.
 3. Cookery (Eggs)--Juvenile literature. 4. Eggs--Juvenile literature. I. Title.
 TX759.H65 2010
 641.6'7--dc22
                                                    2008044532

9 8 7 6 5 4 3 2 1

Contents

Milk

Milk comes from cows. It is sold in plastic cartons and jugs.

Eating grass helps cows to make milk.

4

Milk makes your bones grow strong and stay healthy.

Try to drink milk every day.

5

Milk in Foods

Foods such as butter, cheese, yogurt, and cream are made from milk.

yogurt

milk

cheese

butter

 Foods made from milk are called dairy products.

Butter is spread on bread and toast. It is also used in cooking.

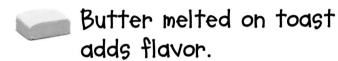

Butter melted on toast adds flavor.

Yogurt

Yogurt is thick and creamy. It is sold in cartons in lots of different flavors.

Yogurt is a healthy snack.

Mix your favorite fruit with a bowl of plain yogurt.

Try yogurt as a topping on cereal or a dessert. You can use yogurt instead of cream.

Hard Cheese

Cheeses such as Edam, cheddar, and Gouda are called hard cheeses.

Edam

Each hard cheese has a different taste.

Gouda

Hard cheese is great in a sandwich or eaten on its own as a snack.

Cheddar cheese

A sandwich with cheese and an apple make a healthy lunch.

Soft Cheese

Creamy cheese that is easy to spread is called soft cheese.

Soft cheese tastes good on crackers.

Cottage cheese is a soft cheese that is sold in a tub. You can eat it with salad, on a baked potato, or by itself.

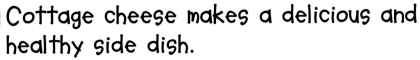 Cottage cheese makes a delicious and healthy side dish.

Cooking with Cheese

Different cheeses are used to make flavorful and sweet dishes.

Cheese is melted to make a sauce for broccoli and cauliflower.

Cheesecake is made by mixing soft cheese with sugar.

Cheesecake can be served with fruit sauce.

15

Eggs

Eggs are laid by female chickens called hens.

 Hens can lay brown or white eggs.

An egg has a shell on the outside. A yellow yolk and egg white are on the inside.

yolk

shell

egg white

 Uncooked eggs are unhealthy to eat.

17

Cooking with Eggs

Many foods have eggs in them. Eggs are used to make pasta, custard, cakes, and desserts.

meringue is made from egg whites

This lemon pie has a meringue topping.

Salad with hard-boiled eggs is easy to make and very good for you.

When eggs are cooked in their shells in boiling water, they become hard. These are called hard-boiled eggs.

Breakfast Eggs

Lots of people have eggs for breakfast. Try them boiled, scrambled, fried, or poached.

Scrambled eggs on toast makes a filling breakfast.

Omelettes are cooked eggs folded over with vegetables, meat, or cheese inside.

Have a ham or vegetable omelette for breakfast.

Things to Do

Cheesy Choice

Can you name these cheeses? Which is cottage cheese? Which is Gouda? Which is Edam?

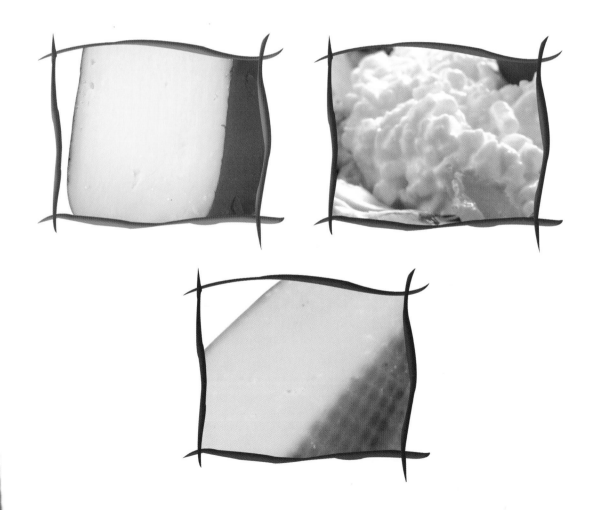

Eggscellent!

Can you match the two halves to find an omelette, scrambled egg on toast, and a boiled egg salad?

Super Sandwich

Which of these foods would make a tasty sandwich filling?

Glossary

dairy foods
These are any foods made from milk such as butter, cheese, yogurt, and cream.

dessert a sweet food, usually served at the end of a meal.

poached
Eggs cooked without their shells, in boiling water.

Index